عشر قواعد
في الاستقامة

TEN PRINCIPLES
ON AL-ISTIQAAMAH

BY SHAYKH 'ABDUR RAZZAAQ BIN
ABDIL-MUHSIN AL-'ABBAD AL-BADR

ISBN: 978-1-4675-1886-4

Cover Design By: www.strictlysunnahdesigns.com

Published by: Maktabatulirshad Publications

Printed by: Ohio Printing

Translation by: Ihsân Ibn Gerald Gonsalves

Revision of Translation by: Aboo Sulaymaan Muhammad
'Abdul Azim Ibn Joshua Baker

Website: www.maktabatulirshad.com

Email: info@maktabatulirshad.com

Subject: Usūl-ul-Deen

مكتبة الإرشاد
Maktabatul-Irshad
PUBLICATIONS

TABLE OF CONTENTS

BRIEF BIOGRAPHY OF THE AUTHOR

<u>His name</u>: Shaykh 'Abdur-Razzaaq Bin 'Abdil-Muhsin Al-'Abbad Al-Badr.

He is the son of Al-'Allamah Muhaddith of Medina Shaykh 'Abdul-Muhsin Al-'Abbad Al-Badr.

<u>Birth</u>: He was born on the 22nd day of Dhul-Qaddah in the year 1382 AH in az-Zal'fi, Kingdom of Saudia Arabia. He currently resides in Al-Medina Al-Munawwarah.

<u>Current occupation</u>: He is a member of the teaching staff in the Islamic University, in Al-Medina.

<u>Scholastic certifications</u>: Doctorate in 'Aqeedah.

The Shaykh has authored books, researches, as well as numerous explanations in different sciences. Among them:

1. Fiqh of Supplications & Ad-Dhkaar.

2. Hajj & refinement of Souls,

3. Explanation of the book "Exemplary Principles" By Shaykh 'Uthaymeen ﷺ (May Allāh have mercy upon him).

4. Explanation of the book "the principles of Names & Attributes" authored by Shaykh-ul-Islam Ibn Qayyum (May Allāh have mercy upon him).

5. Explanation of the book "Good Words" authored by Shaykh-ul-Islam Ibn Qayyum (May Allāh have mercy upon him).
6. Explanation of the book "Aqeedah Tahaawiyyah".
7. Explanation of the book "Fusuul: Biography of the Messenger ﷺ) By Ibn Katheer (May Allāh have mercy upon him).
8. He has a full explanation of the book "Aadaab-ul-Muf'rad" authored by Imam Bukhari (May Allāh have mercy upon him).

From the most distinguished scholars whom he has taken knowledge and acquired knowledge from are:

1. His father Al-'Allamah Shaykh 'Abdul-Muhsin Al-Badr — may Allāh preserve him.

2. Al-'Allamah Shaykh Ibn Baaz — may Allāh have mercy upon him.

3. Al-'Allamah Shaykh Muhammad Bin Saleh Al-'Uthaymeen — may Allāh have mercy upon him.

4. Shaykh 'Ali Nasir Faqeehi — may Allāh preserve him.

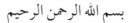

INTRODUCTION

Verily all praise is for Allāh. We seek his aid; we seek his forgiveness and we seek refuge in Allāh from the evil within ourselves and the evil of our actions. Whoever Allāh chooses to guide then he will be guided and whoever Allāh misguides then there will be no guidance for him. I bear witness that there is none worthy of worship except Allāh , alone and with no partners, and I bear witness that Muhammad is His slave and His messenger, may the peace and blessings of Allāh be upon him and his companions

This treatise is about *al-Istiqaamah* (uprightness). This is a topic of great importance and significant magnitude. It is the responsibility of every one of us to give it importance and attention.

Allāh says:

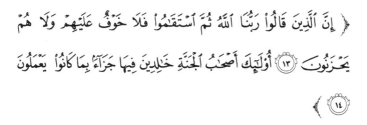

"Verily, those who say: "Our Lord is (only) Allāh ," and thereafter Istaqamu (i.e. stood firm and straight

on the Islamic Faith of Monotheism by abstaining from all kinds of sins and evil deeds which Allāh has forbidden and by performing all kinds of good deeds which He has ordained), on them shall be no fear, nor shall they grieve. Such shall be the dwellers of Paradise; abiding therein (forever), a reward for what they used to do." [1]

Allāh says:

﴿ إِنَّ ٱلَّذِينَ قَالُوا۟ رَبُّنَا ٱللَّهُ ثُمَّ ٱسْتَقَـٰمُوا۟ تَتَنَزَّلُ عَلَيْهِمُ ٱلْمَلَـٰٓئِكَةُ أَلَّا تَخَافُوا۟ وَلَا تَحْزَنُوا۟ وَأَبْشِرُوا۟ بِٱلْجَنَّةِ ٱلَّتِى كُنتُمْ تُوعَدُونَ ۝ نَحْنُ أَوْلِيَآؤُكُمْ فِى ٱلْحَيَوٰةِ ٱلدُّنْيَا وَفِى ٱلْءَاخِرَةِ وَلَكُمْ فِيهَا مَا تَشْتَهِىٓ أَنفُسُكُمْ وَلَكُمْ فِيهَا مَا تَدَّعُونَ ۝ نُزُلًا مِّنْ غَفُورٍ رَّحِيمٍ ۝ ﴾

"Verily, those who say: "Our Lord is Allāh (Alone)," and then they Istaqamu, on them the angels will descend (at the time of their death) (saying): "Fear not, nor grieve! But receive the glad tidings of Paradise which you have been promised! We have been your friends in the life of this world and are (so) in the Hereafter. Therein you shall have (all) that your inner-selves desire, and therein you shall have (all) for which you ask for. An entertainment from (Allāh), the Oft-Forgiving, Most Merciful." [2]

Istiqaamah brings about happiness in the Dunya and the

---

[1] Al-Ah'qaf [46:13-14]
[2] Fussilat [41:30-32]

hereafter, success for the slave and rectification of all his affairs. Therefore, it is the responsibility of the one who wishes to advise oneself and desires the joy of *al-Istiqaamah* to pay it great attention. This is done through knowledge, action and firmness upon that until death and by relying upon the help of Allāh.

A common question for the scholars, students of knowledge, callers to Allāh and the righteous are often concerning *al-Istiqaamah*, its reality, the things that help to be firm upon Allāh's straight path, etc. I thought that it would be beneficial for myself and my brothers in Islâm to gather some of the important and comprehensive principles on this subject; so that they may be a light for us. I gathered these principles after studying the sayings of the people of knowledge (may Allāh have mercy upon them) about *al-Istiqaamah* and that which is connected with it. I shall mention in this treatise 10 great principles concerning the topic of *al-Istiqaamah*. These principles are important for every one of us to pay attention (to).

I rely upon the help of Allāh alone and may Allāh grant me success.

THE 1ST PRINCIPLE: AL-ISTIQAAMAH IS A DIVINE BLESSING AND A GIFT FROM ALLĀH

In many verses from Allāh 's Book He -The Glorified and Most High- connects Himself to the guidance to His straight path. The whole affair is by His hand: He guides whom He wills and misguides whom He wills. By His hand -the Glorified, the Most High- are the hearts of the slaves so whoever He wills he makes him steadfast upon the correct path and whoever He wills He deviates him from it. Allāh the Most High says,

﴿ وَلَوْ أَنَّا كَتَبْنَا عَلَيْهِمْ أَنِ ٱقْتُلُوٓاْ أَنفُسَكُمْ أَوِ ٱخْرُجُواْ مِن دِيَٰرِكُم مَّا فَعَلُوهُ إِلَّا قَلِيلٌ مِّنْهُمْ وَلَوْ أَنَّهُمْ فَعَلُواْ مَا يُوعَظُونَ بِهِۦ لَكَانَ خَيْرًا لَّهُمْ وَأَشَدَّ تَثْبِيتًا ﴿٦٦﴾ وَإِذًا لَّآتَيْنَٰهُم مِّن لَّدُنَّآ أَجْرًا عَظِيمًا ﴿٦٧﴾ وَلَهَدَيْنَٰهُمْ صِرَٰطًا مُّسْتَقِيمًا ﴿٦٨﴾ ﴾

"But if they had done what they were told, it would have been better for them, and would have strengthened their (Faith); And indeed, We should then have bestowed upon them a great reward from Ourselves. And indeed, We should have guided them to a Straight Way (As-Siraat Al-Mustaqim)." [3]

---

[3] An-Nisaa [4:66-68]

Therefore, guidance to the straight path (*As-Siraat Al-Mustaqim*) is in Allāh's hand alone. Allāh the Most High says,

$$﴿ فَأَمَّا ٱلَّذِينَ ءَامَنُواْ بِٱللَّهِ وَٱعۡتَصَمُواْ بِهِۦ فَسَيُدۡخِلُهُمۡ فِى رَحۡمَةٖ مِّنۡهُ وَفَضۡلٖ وَيَهۡدِيهِمۡ إِلَيۡهِ صِرَٰطٗا مُّسۡتَقِيمٗا ١٧٥ ﴾$$

"So, as for those who believed in Allāh and held fast to Him, He will admit them to His Mercy and Grace (i.e. Paradise), and guide them to Himself by a Straight Path." [4]

He says:

$$﴿ وَٱللَّهُ يَدۡعُوٓاْ إِلَىٰ دَارِ ٱلسَّلَٰمِ وَيَهۡدِى مَن يَشَآءُ إِلَىٰ صِرَٰطٖ مُّسۡتَقِيمٖ ٢٥ ﴾$$

"Allāh calls to the home of peace (i.e., Paradise, by accepting Allāh's religion of Islamic Monotheism and by doing righteous good deeds and abstaining from polytheism and evil deeds) and guides whom He wills to a Straight Path." [5]

He says:

$$﴿ وَٱلَّذِينَ كَذَّبُواْ بِـَٔايَٰتِنَا صُمّٞ وَبُكۡمٞ فِى ٱلظُّلُمَٰتِۗ مَن يَشَإِ ٱللَّهُ يُضۡلِلۡهُ$$

---

[4] An-Nisaa [4:175]
[5] Yunus [10:25]

[11]

﴿ ۞ وَمَن يَشَأْ يَجْعَلْهُ عَلَىٰ صِرَٰطٍ مُّسْتَقِيمٍ ﴾

"Those who reject Our Ayât (proofs, evidences, verses, lessons, signs, revelations, etc.) are deaf and dumb in darkness. Allāh sends astray whom He wills and He guides on the Straight Path whom He wills." [6]

He says:

﴿ وَٱللَّهُ يَهْدِى مَن يَشَآءُ إِلَىٰ صِرَٰطٍ مُّسْتَقِيمٍ ۞ ﴾

"And Allāh guides whom He wills to a Straight Path (i.e. to Allāh 's religion of Islamic Monotheism)" [7]

He -the Most High- says:

﴿ إِنْ هُوَ إِلَّا ذِكْرٌ لِّلْعَٰلَمِينَ ۞ لِمَن شَآءَ مِنكُمْ أَن يَسْتَقِيمَ ۞ وَمَا تَشَآءُونَ إِلَّآ أَن يَشَآءَ ٱللَّهُ رَبُّ ٱلْعَٰلَمِينَ ۞ ﴾

"Verily, this (the Quran) is no less than a Reminder to (all) the 'Alamin (mankind and jinns). To whomsoever among you who wills to walk straight, and you will not, unless (it be) that Allāh wills, the Lord of the 'Alamin (mankind, jinns and all that

---

[6] An'aam [6:39]
[7] An-Nur [24:36]

exists)." [8]

There are many verses like these in the Quran. Guidance is by Allāh 's hand. By it, He blesses whom He wills from his slaves. For this reason, it is the first principle of *al-Istiqaamah*. It is based upon seeking *al-Istiqaamah* from Allāh, as it is with his hand - The Glorified, The Most High. He is the guide to the straight path. This was the subject of most of the supplications of the Prophet ﷺ, for example, he said:

يَا مُقَلِّبَ الْقُلُوبِ ثَبِّتْ قَلْبِي عَلَى دِينِكَ

"Oh changer of hearts, make my heart firm upon your religion."

This is firmness upon *al-Istiqaamah*. Umm Salamah said:

يَا رَسُولَ اللهِ ! أَوْ إِنَّ الْقُلُوبَ لَتَتَقَلَّبُ ؟ قَالَ:

((نَعَمْ: مَا مِنْ خَلْقِ اللهِ مِنْ بَنِي آدَمَ مِنْ بَشَرٍ إِلَّا

أَنَّ قَلْبَهُ بَيْنَ أُصْبُعَيْنِ مِنْ أَصَابِعِ اللهِ , فَإِنْ شَاءَ

عَزَّ وَجَلَّ أَقَامَهُ , وَإِنْ شَاءَ أَزَاغَهُ .

"Oh messenger of Allāh! Do the hearts really change?", He said: "Yes, there is not anyone from Allāh 's creation, from the sons of Adam, from mankind, except that his heart is between the two fingers of Allāh. If Allāh wills, he makes him

---

[8] At-Tak'weer [81:27-29]

upright, and if He wills, he deviates him." [9]

Al-Istiqaamah is in the hand of Allāh so whoever wants it for himself then he should seek it from Allāh and persist in asking for it. It is reported in *Sahih Muslim* from the hadith of Aishah (may Allāh be pleased with her) that she was asked:

بِأَيِّ شَيْءٍ كَانَ النَّبِيُّ – صَلَّى اللهُ عَلَيْهِ وَ سَلَّمَ
– يَفْتَتِحُ صَلَاتَهُ مِنَ اللَّيْلِ؟ قَالَتْ: إِذَا قَامَ مِنَ
اللَّيْلِ افْتَتَحَ صَلَاتَهُ: ((اللَّهُمَّ رَبَّ جِبْرِيلَ وَ
مِيكَائِيلَ وَ إِسْرَافِيلَ , فَاطِرَ السَّمَوَاتِ وَ الْأَرْضِ
عَالِمَ الْغَيْبِ وَ الشَّهَادَةِ , أَنْتَ تَحْكُمُ بَيْنَ
عِبَادِكَ فِيمَا كَانُوا فِيهِ يَخْتَلِفُونَ اهْدِنِي لِمَا
اخْتَلَفَتْ فِيهِ مِنَ الْحَقِّ بِإِذْنِكَ إِنَّكَ تَهْدِي مَنْ
تَشَاءُ إِلَى صِرَاطٍ مُسْتَقِيمٍ))

"With what did the Prophet (ﷺ) begin his night prayer? She said: "If he stood for the night prayer he would begin it with: Oh Allāh , lord of Jibra'il, Micha'il and Israfil, creator of the heavens and the earth, knower of the unseen and the testimony and you judge between your slaves in

---

[9] Ahmad noted it #26576. At-Tirmidhi noted it #3522 and graded it to be Hasan. Look in the book *"As-Saheehah"* by Shaykh Al-Albaani #2091.

that which they differ. Guide me in that which I have differed from the truth with your permission. You guide whom you will to the straight path." 10

Therefore, He ﷺ would say every night in the beginning of the night prayer:

إِنَّكَ تَـهْـدِي مَـنْ تَـشَـاءُ إِلَـى صِـرَاطٍ مُـسْـتَـقِـيـمٍ

"Verily you guide whomever you will to the straight path."

This request is of such great importance that Allāh made, upon his servants, obligatory to ask for guidance to the straight path continually day and night in Soorah Fatihah. Allāh says in the opening of His book:

﴿ اهْدِنَا الصِّرَٰطَ الْمُسْتَقِيمَ ۝ صِرَٰطَ الَّذِينَ أَنْعَمْتَ عَلَيْهِمْ غَيْرِ الْمَغْضُوبِ عَلَيْهِمْ وَلَا الضَّالِّينَ ۝ ﴾

"Guide us to the Straight Way. The Way of those on whom you have bestowed Your Grace, not (the way) of those who earned Your Anger (such as the Jews), nor of those who went astray (such as the Christians)." 11

Some of the people of knowledge say that it should be stressed to the general people that it is a supplication when you say:

---

10 Saheeh Muslim #770.
11 Fatihah [1:6-7]

[15]

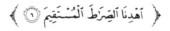

"Guide us to the straight path..."

You are supplicating to Allāh with this supplication that Allāh has made us recite day and night 17 times in each *rakat* of the 5 daily prayers. Therefore, it is important that the Muslim understands that this is a supplication. Sheikh Al-Islam Ibn Taymiyyah (may Allāh have mercy upon) said:

> **"I considered what was the most beneficial supplication, and I found it to be to ask for aid in Allāh 's pleasure, then I saw it in the Fatihah: "You alone we worship and you alone we seek help."** [12]

He said:

> **"The slave is ordered with constant supplication to Allāh, the glorified, for guidance to al-Istiqaamah."** [13]

It is sought, from you, to supplicate continually to Allāh for *al-Istiqaamah,* and it is present in Soorah Fatihah. Al-Hasan Al-Basri used to say when he read the saying of Allāh:

﴿ إِنَّ ٱلَّذِينَ قَالُواْ رَبُّنَا ٱللَّهُ ثُمَّ ٱسۡتَقَٰمُواْ ﴾

"Verily, those who say: "Our Lord is Allāh (Alone),"

---

[12] *"Madaarij Salikeen"* by Ibn-ul-Qayyim (1/78).
[13] *"Iqtidaa' As-Siraat al-Mustaqim" by* Ibn Taymiyah (1/83).

and then they Istaqamu (are upright)." [14]

He says:

"Oh, Allāh you are our lord so bless us with al-Istiqaamah." [15]

---

[14] Fussilat [41:30]
[15] At-Tabari noted it in his Tafsir (21/465).

[17]

THE SECOND PRINCIPLE: THE REALITY OF AL-ISTIQAAMAH IS FOLLOWING THE CORRECT METHODOLOGY AND THE SIRAAT AL-MUSTAQIM (STRAIGHT PATH)

We seek guidance in the reality of *al-Istiqaamah* by considering the blessed sayings of the *Sahaabah* and the *Tabi'een* in regards to the clarification of its meaning and explanation of its reality.

Abu Bakr (may Allāh be pleased with him) said in his explanation of the verse:

﴿ إِنَّ ٱلَّذِينَ قَالُوا۟ رَبُّنَا ٱللَّهُ ثُمَّ ٱسْتَقَٰمُوا۟ ﴾

**"Verily, those who say: "Our Lord is Allāh (Alone),"
and then they Istaqamu (are upright)"**

هُـمُ الَّـذِينَ لَـمْ يُـشَـارِكُوا۟ بِـاللهِ شَـيْـئًا.

**"They are those that never associated any partners
with Allāh."** 16

It has been reported that Umar bin Al-Khattaab (may Allāh be pleased with him) that he read this verse on the *Min'bar*:

---

16 At-Tabari noted in his Tafsir (21/464)

﴿ إِنَّ ٱلَّذِينَ قَالُوا۟ رَبُّنَا ٱللَّهُ ثُمَّ ٱسْتَقَٰمُوا۟ ﴾

"Verily, those who say: "Our Lord is Allāh (Alone),"
and then they Istaqamu (are upright)"

And said:

لَمْ يَرُوغُوا۟ رَوَغَانَ الـثَّعْـلَـبِ

"They are never deceitful like the deceitful fox."

On the authority of Ibn Abbas (may Allāh be pleased with
him) the meaning of "Then Istaqamu (are upright)" is:

عَـلَـى شَـهَـادَةِ أَنْ لَا إِلَـهَ إِلَّا اللهُ

"They are steadfast upon the testification that there
is none worthy of worship except Allaah."

Similar quotes were narrated from Anas, Mujahid,
Al-Aswad bin Hilal, Zaid bin Aslam, As-Siddi and
Ikramah, amongst others. [17] It is also reported on the
authority of Ibn Abbas that he said:

"They are steadfast upon performing the
obligations." [18]

Abu Aliyah said:

"Then make the religion and the actions sincere

---

[17] Look in the book *"Tafsir of At-Tabari"* (21/464-465)
published by *"Risaalah foundation"*.
[18] At-Tabari noted it in his Tafsir (21/465).

[19]

for him." [19]

Qatada said about Allāh's saying: "...then they Istaqamu":

"They are steadfast upon obedience to Allaah." [20]

Ibn Rajab رحمه الله (may Allāh have mercy upon him) mentioned these quotes in his book *"Jami' Al-Uloom wal Hikam"* [21] then he defined *al-Istiqaamah* as,

"The way of the straight path, the correct religion without any corruption. That includes performing all the obedient acts, apparent and hidden, and leaving all the forbidden acts. Therefore, this is a comprehensive commandment for the characteristics of the whole of the religion." [22]

All of these meanings are similar, and they explain each other, because *al-Istiqaamah* is from the comprehensive terms that encompass the whole of the religion. Ibn al-Qayyim رحمه الله said:

"Al-Istiqaamah is a comprehensive term taken from the whole of the religion. It is standing between the hands of Allāh with true honesty and fulfilling the covenant." [23]

---

[19] Al-Maa'wiridi in the book *"An-Nukt wal-'Uyun"* (5/275).
[20] 'Abdur-Razzaaq noted in the," Al-*Musannif*" (2618).
[21] (pg. 384-383)
[22] In the book, *"Jami' Al-Uloom wal Hikam"* (pg. 385).
[23] In the book *"Madaarij Salikeen"* (2/105).

THE THIRD PRINCIPLE: THE FOUNDATION OF AL-ISTIQAAMAH IS UPRIGHTNESS OF THE HEART

Imam Ahmad reported from the hadith of Anas bin Malik (may Allāh be pleased with him) that the Prophet ﷺ said:

لَا يَسْتَقِيمُ إِيمَانُ عَبْدٍ حَتَّى يَسْتَقِيمَ قَلْبُهُ

"The belief of a slave is not upright until his heart is upright." [24]

Therefore, the foundation of *al-Istiqaamah* is *Istiqaamah* of the heart. If the heart is correct and upright, then the body will follow. Al-Hafidh ibn Rajab ﵀ (may Allāh have mercy upon him) said,

"The foundation of al-Istiqaamah is steadfastness (Istiqaamah) of the heart upon Tawheed."

Similarly, Abu Bakr As-Siddiq explained Allāh's verse:

﴿ إِنَّ ٱلَّذِينَ قَالُوا۟ رَبُّنَا ٱللَّهُ ثُمَّ ٱسْتَقَـٰمُوا۟ ﴾

"Verily, those who say: "Our Lord is Allāh (Alone),""

---

[24] Imam Ahmad noted in *"Al-Musnad"* (13048). And Shaykh Al-Albaani graded it to be *Hasan* in his book *"As-Saheehah"* (2841).

and then they Istaqamu (are upright)"

"With that they are the ones who never turned to other than Him. Therefore, when the heart is upright and steadfast (mustaqim) upon the knowledge of Allāh , upon fearing Him, upon His greatness, upon His sublimity, upon His love, upon His will, upon His hope, upon His supplication, trusting in Him and turning away from other than Him then all the limbs will become steadfast upon obedience to Him. The heart is the king of the limbs, and they are his army. If the king is upright, then so will be his army and subjects." [25]

It is reported in the two authentic books of hadith (Bukhari and Muslim) upon the authority of Nu'man bin Bashir (may Allāh be pleased with them both) that he heard the Prophet ﷺ saying:

إِنَّ فِي الْجَسَدِ مُضْغَةً , إِذَا صَلَحَتْ صَلَحَ الْجَسَدُ
كُلُّهُ وَإِذَا فَسَدَتْ فَسَدَ الْجَسَدُ كُلُّهُ أَلَا وَهِيَ الْقَلْبُ

"Verily in the body is an organ if it is correct then the whole body is correct and if it is corrupt then the whole body is corrupt. Verily it is the heart." [26]

Ibn Al-Qayyim ﷺ (may Allāh have mercy upon him) said in the introduction of his book" *Igathatu Al-Lahfan min Masa'id As-Shaytan*" (Aid for the Regretful from the Traps

---

[25] In the book, *"Jami' Al-Uloom wal Hikam"* (pg. 386).
[26] Al-Bukhari (52) and Muslim (1599).

of the Devil):

"The heart is to the limbs like the king is to the army. They do all that they are ordered, and he uses them for whatever he wills. They are under his servitude and his power. They take from him uprightness (Istiqaamah) and deviance. They follow him in that which he is sure or unsure." [27]

The Prophet (ﷺ) said:

إِنَّ فِي الْجَسَدِ مُضْغَةً , إِذَا صَلَحَتْ صَلَحَ الْجَسَدُ كُلُّهُ وَإِذَا فَسَدَتْ فَسَدَ الْجَسَدُ كُلُّهُ أَلَا وَهِيَ الْقَلْبُ

"Verily in the body is an organ if it is correct then the whole body is correct. Verily it is the heart."

The heart is the ruler, and they are the implementers of his orders. They face that which comes to them from its guidance. Nothing of their actions will be upright until they originate from its intentions, and it is responsible for them. Allāh ﷻ -The Almighty, The Most High- says:

﴿ يَوْمَ لَا يَنفَعُ مَالٌ وَلَا بَنُونَ ۝ إِلَّا مَنْ أَتَى اللَّهَ بِقَلْبٍ سَلِيمٍ ۝ ﴾

"The Day whereon neither wealth nor sons will avail. Except him who brings to Allāh a clean heart [clean from Shirk (polytheism) and Nifaaq

---

[27] In the book, "Igathatu Al-Lahfan min Masa'id As-Shaytan" (1/5).

(hypocrisy)]" [28]

...and the Prophet ﷺ used to make the supplication:

اللَّـهُـمَّ إِنِّـي أَسْـأَ لُـكَ قَـلْـبًا سَـلِـيـمًا

"*Oh Allāh I ask you for a pure heart.*" [29]

---

[28] Ash-Shuraa' [26:88-89]
[29] Imam Ahmad noted it (17114). And An-Nasaaee' (1304).
Look in the book *"As-Saheehah"* (2328).

THE FOURTH PRINCIPLE: THE ISTIQAAMAH THAT IS SOUGHT FROM THE SLAVE IS AS-SADDAD AND IF HE IS NOT ABLE THEN AL-MAQARIBAH

The Prophet ﷺ grouped these two affairs (*as-saddad* and *almaqaribah*) together in his saying:

إِنَّ الدِّينَ يُسْرٌ وَلَنْ يُشَادَّ الدِّينَ أَحَدٌ إِلَّا غَلَبَهُ فَسَدِّدُواْ وَقَارِبُواْ وَأَبْشِرُوا

"Verily the religion is ease. No one will ever make the religion difficult except it will overcome him. So saddidu and qaaribu and receive the glad tidings." [30]

Therefore, that, which is sought for in regards to *al-Istiqaamah,* is *as-saddad. As-saddad* is to perform the *Sunnah* completely. The Prophet ﷺ (may peace and blessings be upon him) said to Ali (may Allāh be pleased with him) when he asked him to teach him a supplication, he said:

قُلْ: اللَّهُمَّ اِهْدِنِي وَ سَدِّدْنِي. قَالَ:((وَاذْكُرْ بِالْهُدَى هِدَايَتَكَ الطَّرِيقَ , وَ السَّدَادِ سَدَادَ

---

[30] Bukhari noted (39 & 6463) from the hadith of Abi Hurairah ☐ .

[25]

((السَّهْم))

*" Say: Oh Allāh guide me and saddidny (make me
from those that perform the Sunnah completely)",
he said: "...and mention guidance when you are lost
and as-saddad when you want your arrow to be on
target."* [31]

The servant is required to struggle with himself to attain
as-saddad, to follow the guidance of the Prophet ﷺ,
his way, and his mannerisms. A person must strive upon
that, and if he is unable then he must try to come close to
that (*maqariba*). Allāh the most high says:

$$﴿ فَٱسْتَقِيمُوٓا۟ إِلَيْهِ وَٱسْتَغْفِرُوهُ ﴾$$

*"...therefore, take the Straight Path to Him (with
true Faith Islamic Monotheism and obedience) to
Him, and seek forgiveness of Him."* [32]

The mentioning of forgiveness after the order for *Istiqaamah*
shows that the servant will inevitably fall short whenever
he strives for *al-Istiqaamah*. This is the reason why
Al-Hafidh ibn Rajab ﷺ (may Allāh have mercy upon
him) said:

"In His -The All Powerful, the Most Venerable's- saying:

---

[31] Muslim noted it (2725).
[32] Fussilat [41:6]

[26]

﴿ فَٱسْتَقِيمُوٓاْ إِلَيْهِ وَٱسْتَغْفِرُوهُ ﴾

"...therefore, take the Straight Path to Him (with true Faith Islamic Monotheism and obedience) to Him, and seek forgiveness of Him."

There is an indication that it is inevitable to fall short of the *Istiqaamah* with that we have been ordered. Therefore, that is restored by seeking forgiveness, which mandates repentance and returning to *al-Istiqaamah*. It is like the saying of the Prophet ﷺ to Muadh:

اِتَّقِ اللهَ حَيْثُ مَا كُنْتَ , وَ أَتْبِعِ السَّيِّئَةَ الْحَسَنَةَ تَمْحُهَا .

"Fear Allāh wherever you are and follow a bad deed with a good deed to wipe it away."

The Prophet ﷺ) informs us that people will never be able to achieve the true *Istiqaamah*. Imam Ahmad and Ibn Majah reported from the hadith of Thaw'ban that the Prophet ﷺ said:

اسْتَقِيمُوٓاْ وَ لَنْ تُحْصُواْ , واعْلَمُواْ أَنَّ خَيْرَ أَعْمَالِكُمُ الصَّلَاةُ , وَ لَا يُحَافِظُ عَلَى الْوُضُوءِ إِلَّا مُؤْمِنٌ

"Istaqimu (be upright) but you will never encapsulate (it completely) and know that the best action is the prayer and only the believer is diligent

upon performing the wudoo (ablutions)." [33]

And in Imam Ahmad's wording:

$$\text{سَـدِّدُواْ وَ قَارِبُـواْ وَ لَا يُحَافِظُ عَلَى الْـوُضُـوءِ إِلَّا مُـؤْمِـنٌ}$$

"Saddidu (perform the Sunnah completely) and
qaaribu (do that which you are able from the
Sunnah) and only the believer is diligent upon
performing the wudoo." (ablutions)." [34]

Narrated also in Bukhari and Muslim on the authority of
Abu Hurayrah (may Allāh be pleased with him) that the
Prophet ﷺ said:

$$\text{سَـدِّدُواْ وَ قَارِبُـواْ}$$

'Saddidu (perform the Sunnah completely) and
qaaribu (do that which you are able from the
Sunnah)'. [35]

As-saddad is the reality of *al-Istiqaamah*. It is to be correct in
all of your speech, actions and intentions, like the one who
shoots at a target and hits it. The Prophet ﷺ ordered

---

[33] Musnad Imam Ahmad (22378) and Sunan Ibn Majah
(277). Shaykh Al-Albaani authenticated it in his book
"Irwaa' al-Ghaleel" (412).
[34] Musnad Imam Ahmad (22432).
[35] Bukhari noted it (6463); and Muslim noted it (2816, 76).

Ali to ask Allāh ﷻ -The Almighty, The Most Venerable- for *as-saddad* and guidance and he said to him:

$$ اُذْكُرْ بِالـسَّـدَادِ تَـسْـدِيـدَكَ الـسَّـهْـمَ , وَ بِالْـهُـدَى هِـدَايَـتَـكَ الـطَّـرِيـقَ . $$

"Mention with 'as-saddad accuracy for your arrow and mention guidance for your guidance to the right path." [36]

Al-maqaribah is to hit close to the target without actually hitting the target itself. Although, this is with the condition that the person's intent is for *as-saddad* and achieving the goal, so the *maqaribah* results unintentionally.

The proof for this is the saying of the Prophet ﷺ :

$$ يَا أَيُّهَا الـنَّـاسُ ! إِنَّـكُمْ لَنْ تَـعْـمَـلُـوا - أَوْ لَنْ تُـطِيـقُـوا - كُلَّ مَا أَمَـرْتُـكُمْ , وَ لَـكِنْ سَـدِّدُوا وَ أَبْـشِـرُواْ . $$

"O mankind you will never do (or never be capable of doing) everything you have been ordered with but saddidu and qaaribu." [37]

"The meaning being intend *at-tasdeed* (completing and performing all of the *Sunnah*), to be perfect and

---

[36] Imam Muslim noted as previously mentioned.
[37] Abu Dawud noted it (1096), Imam Ahmad noted it (17856); and Shaykh Al-Albaani graded it *Hasan* in his book *"Irwaa' Ghaleel"* (616).

THE FOURTH PRINCIPLE: THE ISTIQAAMAH THAT IS SOUGHT FROM THE SLAVE IS AS-SADDAD AND IF HE IS NOT ABLE THEN AL-MAQARIBAH

al-Istiqaamah. If they are perfect in all their actions, then they will have completed all that they were ordered to do."
38

---

38 Quote from the book *"Jaami Al-Uloom wal-Hikam"* (1/510-511).

THE FIFTH PRINCIPLE: AL-ISTIQAAMAH IS RELATED TO SPEECH, ACTIONS AND INTENTIONS

The *Istiqaamah* that is sought from the servant is *Istiqaamah* of the speech, actions and intentions. Meaning that the speech of the servant, his limbs and his heart should all act upon *al-Istiqaamah*. Ibn Al-Qayyim ﷽ said in his book "*Madaarij As-Salikeen*":

"**Al-Istiqaamah is concerned with the speech, actions, situations, and intentions."** [39]

Imam Ahmad reports in his book "*Al-Musnad*" from the hadith of Anas (may Allāh be pleased with him) that the Prophet ﷺ said:

لَا يَسْتَقِيمُ إِيمَانُ عَبْدٍ حَتَّى يَسْتَقِيمَ قَلْبُهُ
, وَلَا يَسْتَقِيمُ قَلْبُهُ حَتَّى يَسْتَقِيمَ لِسَانُهُ

"**The belief of the servant will not be upon Istiqaamah until his heart is upon Istiqaamah and his heart will not be upon Istiqaamah until his tongue is upon Istiqaamah."** [40]

Ibn Rajab ﷽ said:

"**The greatest thing that takes care of al-Istiqaamah**

---

[39] In the book "Madaarij Salikeen (2/105).
[40] Its reference was previously mentioned.

after the heart is the tongue. It is the translator and interpreter of the heart." [41]

Here, we must take note of the danger of the heart and tongue upon the servant in regards to *al-Istiqaamah* and deviating away from it. Some of the people of knowledge say:

"A man is by his two small parts: his heart and his tongue."

The heart and tongue are two very small bodily parts, yet the limbs are all subservient to them. If the heart is upright and the tongue is upright then too will be the limbs.

The proof for the heart is the hadith of Nu'man bin Bashir (may Allāh be pleased with him) that was previously mentioned:

أَلَا وَ إِنَّ فِي الْجَسَدِ مُضْغَةً , إِذَا صَلَحَتْ ,
صَلَحَ الْجَسَدُ كُلُّهُ , وَ إِذَا فَسَدَتْ فَسَدَ
الْجَسَدُ كُلُّهُ , أَلَا وَ هِيَ الْقَلْبُ .

"Verily in the body is an organ. If it is correct then the whole body will be correct, and if it is ruined then the whole body is ruined. Verily it is the heart."

The proof for the tongue as reported by At-Tirmidhi from the hadith of Abi Saeed Al-Khudri (may Allāh be pleased

---

with him) that the Prophet ﷺ said:

إِذَا أَصْبَحَ ابْنُ آدَمَ فَإِنَّ الْأَعْضَاءَ كُلَّهَا تُكَفِّرُ اللِّسَانَ, فَتَقُولُ: اتَّقِ اللهَ فِينَا فَإِنَّمَا نَحْنُ بِكَ فَإِنِ اسْتَقَمْتَ اسْتَقَمْنَا وَ إِنِ اعْوَجَجْتَ اعْوَجَجْنَا

"When the son of Adam awakes all his limbs implore the tongue, they say: "Fear Allāh in regards to us, for verily we can only follow you. If you are upright, we are upright. If you are deviant, then we too are deviant." [42]

So, if, the heart is upright then so will be the limbs, and if the tongue is upright then so will be the limbs. The tongue is the translator for the heart and its *khalifah* for the visible parts of the body. When the heart is supported by the tongue the order is carried out. The tongue follows the heart and the limbs follow them both. This is the reason why it is obligatory upon the Muslim to take care of the rectification of his heart and to ask his Lord -The Blessed, The Most High- to rectify and remove the illnesses, disease and blackness from the heart. Then he should work on rectifying his tongue with pure speech and his limbs with righteous actions.

---

[42] At-tirmidhi noted it (2407) and Shaykh Al-Albaani graded it to be *Hasan* in his book *"Saheeh-ul-Targheeb"* (2871).

THE SIXTH PRINCIPLE: THERE IS NO ISTIQAAMAH EXCEPT FOR ALLĀH , WITH ALLĀH   AND UPON THE COMMAND OF ALLĀH

1. For Allāh: (i.e. sincerely for Him), meaning, the servant is upright and follows Allāh 's straight path, being sincerely devoted, by way of that, in all matters for Allāh ﷻ, seeking His reward and His pleasure. Allāh -The Most High- said:

$$ ﴿ وَمَآ أُمِرُوٓاْ إِلَّا لِيَعْبُدُواْ ٱللَّهَ مُخْلِصِينَ لَهُ ٱلدِّينَ ﴾ $$

"And they were commanded not, but that they should worship Allāh, and worship none but Him Alone (abstaining from ascribing partners to Him)."
43

2. With Allāh: i.e. aided by Him upon the realization of, performing of and firmness upon *al-Istiqaamah*. Allāh -The Blessed, The Most High- says:

$$ ﴿ فَٱعْبُدْهُ وَتَوَكَّلْ عَلَيْهِ ﴾ $$

"So, worship Him (O Muhammad) and put your

---

43 Bayyinah [98:5]

[34]

trust in Him." [44]

And:

$$ ﴿ إِيَّاكَ نَعْبُدُ وَإِيَّاكَ نَسْتَعِينُ ۝ ﴾ $$

"You (Alone) we worship, and you (Alone) we ask for help (for each and everything)." [45]

And in the authentic hadith:

$$ اِحْرِصْ عَلَى مَا يَنْفَعُكَ وَاسْتَعِنْ بِالله $$

"Persevere on that which benefits you and seek the aid of Allaah." [46]

3. Upon the command of Allāh: i.e. to continue upon *al-Istiqaamah* in the correct manner, and to continue on the straight path with what Allāh has ordered his servants. Allāh the Most High says,

$$ ﴿ فَٱسْتَقِمْ كَمَآ أُمِرْتَ ﴾ $$

"So, stand (ask Allāh to make) you (Muhammad) firm and straight (on the religion of Islamic Monotheism) as you were commanded." [47]

Some narrations from the *Salaf* (may Allāh have mercy

---

[44] Hud [11:123]
[45] Fatihah [1:5]
[46] Imam Muslim noted (2664) from the hadith of Abi Hurairah.
[47] Hud [11:112]

upon them) have already been mentioned in agreement with this meaning. For example, the saying of Ibn Abbas in regards to the verse

"Then Istaqimu" means be upright in performing the obligatory actions"

Al-Hasan said:

> **"Be upright upon the command of Allāh, so act with obedience to Him and keep away from disobedience to Him."**

The command of Allāh -The Almighty, The Most Venerable- is His *shariah* (law) that He sent with His Prophet ﷺ .

THE SEVENTH PRINCIPLE: IT IS UPON THE SERVANT NO MATTER HOW MUCH HE BECOMES UPRIGHT THAT HE SHOULD NOT DEPEND UPON HIS ACTIONS

It is obligatory upon the servant that he is not content with his actions; no matter how much he becomes righteous and upright, and he should not be amazed with his own worship, or with the abundance of his remembrance of Allāh or other than that from the types of obedience. Ibn Al-Qayyim 🕮 said in this regard:

"That, which is sought from the servant, is al-Istiqaamah, and that is as-saddad. If he is not able to do that, then it is al-maqaribah, and if he does less than that then it is negligence and waste. As was narrated in Bukhari and Muslim from the hadith of Aishah (may Allāh be pleased with her) that the Prophet ﷺ said:

"Saddidu and qaaribu and receive the glad tidings, for verily no one will enter Jannah by his actions." They said: "Even you oh Messenger of Allāh !?" He said: "Even me, unless Allāh envelops me with his forgiveness and mercy." [48]

In this hadith, the Messenger combined all aspects of the religion. He ordered with *al-Istiqaamah* which is *as-saddad* and perfecting the intentions, sayings and actions. He also informs us in the hadith of Thaw'ban:

---

[48] Bukhari noted it (6467); and Muslim (2818).

اِسْتَقِيمُوا وَ لَنْ تُحْصُوا , وَاعْلَمُوا أَنَّ خَيْرَ
أَعْمَالِكُمُ الصَّلَاةُ

"Istaqimu (be upright) though you will never encompass all of it and know that the best of actions is the prayer.",

(He informs us) that they will never be able to truly be upright, so he directs us towards *al-maqaribah*.

Al-maqaribah is to be as close to *Istiqaamah* as one is able, like the one who fires towards a target. If he misses, then he tries to be close to it. Therefore, the Prophet ﷺ informs them:

"that al-Istiqaamah and al-maqaribah will not save anyone on the Day of Judgment. So, let no one be content with his actions, nor they be amazed by them, and let them not see their actions as their saviour. Verily a person will only be saved by the mercy, pardon and excellence of Allāh." [49]

---

[49] Quoted from the book *"Madaarij Salikeen"* (2/105).

THE EIGHTH PRINCIPLE: THE FRUITS OF AL-ISTIQAAMAH IN THIS LIFE AND AL-ISTIQAAMAH UPON THE SIRAAT ON THE DAY OF JUDGMENT

Whoever is guided in this life to Allāh's straight path then he will be guided in the hereafter to the straight path that crosses over the hellfire.

On the day of judgment, a path is laid over the mouth of the hellfire. A path, that is sharper than a knife and thinner than a strand of hair. The people will be ordered to cross it, and their crossings will differ depending on their actions and their uprightness on Allāh's straight path in this life.

Ibn Al-Qayyim [50] ﷽ said:

" **Whoever is guided in this life to Allāh's straight way, the way that He sent His messengers with and sent down his books for, then he will be guided to the straight path in the next life, the path that leads to Jannah, the place of his reward.**"

The servant's firmness on the path in this life decides their firmness upon the path that passes over the mouth of the hellfire in the hereafter. The servants advance upon this path decides his advancement upon that path. There will be those that cross it like lightning; those that cross it like the blink of an eye; those that cross it like the wind; those that cross it like a difficult journey; those that run across; those that walk across and those that crawl across. Some

---

[50] Quoted from the book *"Madaarij Salikeen"* (1/10).

are clawed at, some unimpaired. Some of them are heaped upon one another in the hellfire. The servant should know his movement on that *Siraat* from his movement on this *Siraat* step for step. Allāh says:

$$\text{﴿ هَلْ تُجْزَوْنَ إِلَّا مَا كُنتُمْ تَعْمَلُونَ ۝ ﴾}$$

"Are you being recompensed anything except what you used to do?" [51]

Let him look at his doubts and desires that cripple him from his progression on this straight path. For they are the hooks that sit on either side of that straight path snatching at him and hindering his progress and if they are numerous and strong so will they be in the hereafter. Allāh says,

$$\text{﴿ وَمَا رَبُّكَ بِظَلَّامٍ لِّلْعَبِيدِ ۝ ﴾}$$

"...and your Lord is not at all unjust to (His) slaves."[52]

Whoever was pulled away from the straight path by doubts and desires in this life then the hooks that wait on either side of the path in the hereafter will also pull at them like their doubts and desires did in the *Dunya*. Ibn Al-Qayyim mentioned similar to this also in his book

---

[51] An-Naml [27:90]
[52] Fussilat [41:46]

"Al-Jawab Al-Kafi" (The Comprehensive Reply). [53]

THE NINTH PRINCIPLE: THE OBSTACLES TO AL-ISTIQAAMAH: THE DOUBTS OF MISGUIDANCE AND THE DESIRES OF TRANSGRESSION

Doubts and desires are definitive obstacles preventing from *al-Istiqaamah* and Allāh's straight path. A person continues upon his doubts and desires, and they lead him away from Allāh's straight path. Therefore, every person that deviates from *al-Istiqaamah* does so either by way of desire or doubt. Desire is corruption of actions and doubt is corruption of knowledge. Allāh ﷻ -The Almighty, The Most Venerable- says:

﴿ وَأَنَّ هَٰذَا صِرَٰطِى مُسْتَقِيمًا فَٱتَّبِعُوهُ وَلَا تَتَّبِعُواْ ٱلسُّبُلَ فَتَفَرَّقَ بِكُمْ عَن سَبِيلِهِۦ ﴾

"And verily, this is my Straight Path, so follow it, and follow not (other) paths, for they will separate you away from His Path." [54]

It is reported in Imam Ahmad's "*Musnad*" from the hadith of Abdullah bin Mas'ood that he said:

---

[54] Al-An'aam [6:153]

خَطَّ لَنَا رَسُولُ اللهِ – صَلَّى اللهُ عَلَيْهِ وَ سَلَّمَ –
خَطًّا , ثُمَّ قَالَ : هَذَا سَبِيلُ اللهِ , ثُمَّ خَطَّ
خُطُوطًا عَنْ يَمِينِهِ وَ عَنْ شِمَالِهِ , ثُمَّ قَالَ :
هَذِهِ سُبُلُ عَلَى كُلِّ سَبِيلٍ مِنْهَا شَيْطَانٌ
يَدْعُو إِلَيْهِ , ثُمَّ قَرَأَ ﴿ وَأَنَّ هَذَا صِرَطِى مُسْتَقِيمًا
فَاتَّبِعُوهُ وَلَا تَتَّبِعُوا السُّبُلَ فَتَفَرَّقَ بِكُمْ عَن سَبِيلِهِ ﴾

"The Messenger of Allāh drew a line and said:
"This is the way of Allāh." Then he drew lines on
its left and its right and said: "These are (other)
ways, upon every way there is a devil calling to it."
Then he read "And verily, this is my Straight Path,
so follow it, and follow not (other) paths, for they
will separate you away from His Path." [55]

The devil that calls to deviation from the straight path do
so by calling to doubt or to desires. So, if, they see in a
person negligence then they tempt him with desires, and if
they see he is diligent and protective then they tempt him
with doubts. Some of the Salaf used to say:

"Allāh did not order with something except that
the Shaytan had for it two evil temptations: either
laziness and falling short, or exceeding the
boundaries and extremism, and he does not care

---

[55] Imam Ahmad noted it in his *Musnad* (4142).

which succeeds." [56]

Ibn Al-Qayyim رحمه الله said:

> "**Most of the people fall into these two valleys
> except a very small minority: the valley of falling
> short and the valley of extremism and a very small
> minority are upon the way that the Messenger of
> Allāh and his companions were upon.**"

Here, it is appropriate to bring a magnificent example that
is extremely beneficial, as is authenticated in "*Al-Musnad*",
"*Al-Tirmidhi*", and others, from the hadith of Nawas bin
Sam'an (may Allāh be pleased with him) that the
Messenger of Allāh ﷺ said:

ضَرَبَ اللهُ مَثَلًا صِرَاطًا مُسْتَقِيمًا , وَ عَلَى
جَنْبَتَيِ الصِّرَاطِ سُورَانِ , فِيهِمَا أَبْوَابٌ
مُفَتَّحَةٌ , وَ عَلَى الْأَبْوَابِ سُتُورٌ مُرْخَاةٌ , وَ
عَلَى بَابِ الصِّرَاطِ دَاعٍ يَقُولُ: أَيُّهَا النَّاسُ!
أُدْخُلُوا الصِّرَاطَ جَمِيعًا , وَ لَا تَتَعَرَّجُوا , وَ
دَاعٍ يَدْعُو مِنْ فَوْقِ الصِّرَاطِ , فَإِذَا أَرَادَ يَفْتَحُ
شَيْئًا مِنْ تِلْكَ الْأَبْوَابِ , قَالَ: وَيْحَكَ لَا
تَفْتَحْهُ , فَإِنَّكَ إِنْ تَفْتَحْهُ تَلِجْهُ , وَ الصِّرَاطُ

---

[56] In the book "*Agatha al-Lahfan*" (1/136).

[44]

: الْإِسْلَامُ , وَ السُّورَانِ : حُـدُودُ اللهِ , وَ الْأَبْـوَابُ

الْـمُـفَـتَّـحَـةُ : مَـحَـارِمُ اللهِ , وَ ذَلِكَ الـدَّاعِي عَـلَى

رَأْسِ الـصِّـرَاطِ : كِـتَـابُ اللهِ , وَ الـدَّاعِي مِنْ فَـوْقِ

الـصِّـرَاطِ : وَاعِظُ اللهِ فِي قَـلْـبِ كُـلِّ مُـسْـلِـمٍ .

"Allāh makes the example of a straight path, on either side of it, there are two walls and in those walls are doors and upon the doors are loose curtains. At the gate of the pathway, there is a caller saying: O mankind enter the pathway and do not deviate from it', and at the top of the pathway is a caller who says whenever someone wants to open one of the doors: 'Warning! Do not open it. If you open it, you will enter it'. The pathway is Islam; the walls are the boundaries set by Allāh , the open doors are the things Allāh forbade, the caller at the gateway of the path is the Book of Allāh and the caller at the top of the pathway is the conscience in the heart of every Muslim." [57]

Allāh makes an example to benefit you. Allāh makes an example of a straight path on the left and right of it are walls. In the walls are many doors that you pass on your right and left. Upon the doors are light curtains and as you know the door that is covered with a curtain is not the same as a door with a lock and key; the door with a curtain can

---

[57] Imam Ahmad noted it (17634), At-Tirmidhi noted it (2859), and Al-Haakim noted (1/144) and he authenticated it; and Imam Adh-Dhahabi agreed. Shaykh Al-Albaani as well as in his book "Saheeh-ul-Jaami" (3887).

be entered without any difficulty or obstruction. The upright Muslim who wants to enter into desire finds his heart become tight, unsure and nervous, and this is the conscience that Allāh places in the heart of every Muslim.

The important thing to note from this hadith is that on either side of the way of al-Istiqaamah are doors that take a person in general to two things: doubts or desires. The servant leaves from al-Istiqaamah either from doubts or desires. Ibn Al-Qayyim ﷺ (may Allāh have mercy upon him) said:

وَ قَدْ نَصَبَ اللهُ – سُبْحَانَهُ - الْجَسَرَ الَّذِي
يَمُرُّ النَّاسُ مِنْ فَوْقِهِ إِلَى الْجَنَّةِ , وَ نَصَبَ
بِجَانِبَيْهِ كَلَالِيبَ تَخْطِفُ النَّاسَ
بِأَعْمَالِهِمْ , فَهَكَذَا كَلَالِيبُ الْبَاطِلِ مِنْ
تَشْبِيهَاتِ الضَّلَالِ , وَ شَهَوَاتِ الْغَيِّ تَمْنَعُ
صَاحِبَهَا مِنَ الْإِسْتِقَامَةِ عَلَى طَرِيقِ الْحَقِّ وَ
سُلُوكِهِ , وَالْمَعْصُومُ مَنْ عَصَمَهُ اللهُ .

"Allāh laid a bridge that people will cross over to reach Jannah. And he placed on either side of it hooks that snatch at the people due to their bad deeds. The hooks prevent those that have doubts and follow their desires from Istiqaamah upon the way of truth. And the infallible are those that Allāh

made infallible." [58]

The servant requires two types of guidance to make their progress secure: guidance to the straight path and guidance on the straight path. Ibn Al-Qayyim رحمه الله said:

"Guidance to the path is one thing and guidance on that same path is something else. Do not you see that a man can know the way of a certain country yet he is not good at behaving that way. His behaviour needs guidance in their particular way. For example, travelling at a certain time, taking money by a certain currency and specific amount, settling in a certain area, etc. This guidance is in the way of acting itself. Someone who knows that the way of country is a certain way could neglect that and not reach what is wanted." [59]

---

[58] In the book, "As-Sawaai'q Al-Mursalah" (4/1256).
[59] In the book, "Ibn Qayyim's letter to one of his brothers" (pg. 9).

THE TENTH PRINCIPLE: IMITATING THE DISBELIEVERS IS FROM THE GREATEST REASONS FOR TURNING AWAY FROM AL-ISTIQAAMAH

Imitation of the disbelievers goes back to two types of corrupt acts: corruption of knowledge and corruption of actions. This meaning can be deduced from Allāh's saying:

﴿ اَهْدِنَا الصِّرَاطَ الْمُسْتَقِيمَ ۝ صِرَطَ الَّذِينَ أَنْعَمْتَ عَلَيْهِمْ غَيْرِ الْمَغْضُوبِ

عَلَيْهِمْ وَلَا الضَّآلِّينَ ۝ ﴾

"Guide us to the Straight Way. The Way of those on whom You have bestowed Your Grace, not (the way) of those who earned Your Anger (such as the Jews), nor of those who went astray (such as the Christians)." [60]

Corruption of the Jews came from their actions and corruption of the Christians came from their knowledge. The Jews had knowledge yet did not act upon it, and the Christians acted without knowledge.

Therefore, the corruption that is found in conjunction with *al-Istiqaamah* is either from imitation of the Jews by a person

---

[60] Fatihah [1:6-7]

having knowledge but does not act upon it, or from imitation of the Christians by a person acting without any knowledge or clarity.

Ibn Taymiyyah named his book *"Requirement of the Siraat Al-Mustaqim: Differing from the People of the Hellfire"* [61]. In it, he indicated to some affairs of the People of the Book that this Ummah was tested with, so that the Muslim may protect themselves from deviation from the straight path to the path of those that earned Allāh 's anger or the path of the misguided. In his book, he mentioned the saying of Allāh,

$$ \{ \ \text{وَدَّ كَثِيرٌ مِّنْ أَهْلِ ٱلْكِتَبِ لَوْ يَرُدُّونَكُم مِّنْ بَعْدِ} $$

$$ \text{إِيمَنِكُمْ كُفَّارًا حَسَدًا مِّنْ عِندِ أَنفُسِهِم مِّنْ بَعْدِ مَا نَبَيَّنَ لَهُمُ} $$

$$ \text{ٱلْحَقُّ} \ \} $$

"Many of the people of the Scripture (Jews and Christians) wish that if they could turn you away as disbelievers after you have believed, out of envy from their own selves, even, after the truth (that Muhammad Peace be upon him is Allāh 's Messenger) has become manifest unto them" [62]

He then said:

"So, Allāh dispraised the Jews for their envy of the guidance and knowledge of the believers. He tested

---

those that had some knowledge with jealousy for those that Allāh had guided with beneficial knowledge and righteous deeds. Jealousy is a characteristic that is generally dispraised, but in this situation, it is one of the characteristics of those that earned the anger of Allāh."

He ﷺ then begins to mention a number of examples of things that are from the actions of the Jews and the Christians that some of the Muslims have imitated. The Prophet ﷺ said:

لَتَتْبَعُنَّ سَنَنَ مَنْ كَانَ قَبْلَكُمْ شِبْراً شِبْراً

وَ ذِرَاعًا بِذِرَاعٍ حَتَّى لَوْ دَخَلُواْ جُحْرَ ضَبٍّ

تَبِعْتُمُوهُمْ

"You shall follow the ways of those that came before you hand span for hand span, forearm for forearm, to the point that if they entered the hole of a lizard then you would follow them." 63

---

63 Imam Bukhari noted it (7320) and Muslim (2669) from the hadith of Abi Saeed Al-Khudri.

CONCLUSION

I conclude with a beautiful quote from Sheikh Al-Islam Ibn Taymiyah (may Allāh have mercy upon him). Ibn Al-Qayyim ﷫ (may Allāh have mercy upon him) said:

"I heard Shaykh Al-Islam Ibn Taymiyah ﷫ (may Allāh have mercy upon him) say:

أَعْظَمُ الْكِرَامَةِ لَزُومُ الْإِسْتِقَامَةِ.

"The greatest al-kiramah (nobility) is the following of al-Istiqaamah." [64]

And Sheikh Al-Islam ﷫ (may Allāh have mercy upon him) in his book *"Al-Furqan bayna Awliyah Al-Rahman and Awliyah As-Shaytan"* (The Criterion between the Allies of The Most Merciful and Allies of the Devil) said:

"The peak of al-kiramah (nobility) is following al-Istiqaamah." [65]

Ibn Al-Qayyim ﷫ narrated from some of the people of knowledge:

"Be an individual of Istiqaamah (uprightness), not a seeker of al-kirama (nobility and stature). For verily, you are active in your search for al-kirama,

---

[64] In the book *"Madaarij Salikeen"* (2/105).
[65] (pg. 349).

but your Lord seeks from you al-Istiqaamah." [66]

This means that the servant must always be striving to follow the straight path and be steadfast upon obedience to Allāh -The Blessed, The Most High- so that he may achieve the greatest of victories. This is the meaning of our Lord's saying:

$$﴿ إِنَّ ٱلَّذِينَ قَالُوا۟ رَبُّنَا ٱللَّهُ ثُمَّ ٱسْتَقَٰمُوا۟ تَتَنَزَّلُ عَلَيْهِمُ ٱلْمَلَٰٓئِكَةُ أَلَّا تَخَافُوا۟ وَلَا تَحْزَنُوا۟ وَأَبْشِرُوا۟ بِٱلْجَنَّةِ ٱلَّتِى كُنتُمْ تُوعَدُونَ ۝ نَحْنُ أَوْلِيَآؤُكُمْ فِى ٱلْحَيَوٰةِ ٱلدُّنْيَا وَفِى ٱلْأَخِرَةِ وَلَكُمْ فِيهَا مَا تَشْتَهِىٓ أَنفُسُكُمْ وَلَكُمْ فِيهَا مَا تَدَّعُونَ ۝ نُزُلًا مِّنْ غَفُورٍ رَّحِيمٍ ۝ ﴾$$

"Verily, those who say: 'Our Lord is Allāh (Alone)', and then they Istaqamu, on them the angels will descend (at the time of their death) (saying): 'Fear not, nor grieve! But receive the glad tidings of Paradise which you have been promised! We have been your friends in the life of this world and are (so) in the Hereafter." Therein you shall have (all) that your inner-selves desire, and therein you shall have (all) for which you ask for. An entertainment from (Allāh), the Oft-Forgiving, Most Merciful." [67]

And His ﷻ saying:

---

[66] "Madaarij Salikeen" (2/105).
[67] Fussilat [41:30-32]

﴿ إِنَّ ٱلَّذِينَ قَالُوا۟ رَبُّنَا ٱللَّهُ ثُمَّ ٱسْتَقَٰمُوا۟ فَلَا خَوْفٌ عَلَيْهِمْ وَلَا هُمْ يَحْزَنُونَ ۞ أُو۟لَٰٓئِكَ أَصْحَٰبُ ٱلْجَنَّةِ خَٰلِدِينَ فِيهَا جَزَآءًۢ بِمَا كَانُوا۟ يَعْمَلُونَ ۞ ﴾

" Verily, those who say: 'Our Lord is (only) Allāh ', and thereafter Istaqamu (i.e. stood firm and straight on the Islamic Faith of Monotheism by abstaining from all kinds of sins and evil deeds which Allāh has forbidden and by performing all kinds of good deeds which He has ordained), on them shall be no fear, nor shall they grieve. Such shall be the dwellers of Paradise, abiding therein (forever), a reward for what they used to do." [68]

I ask Allāh , The Most Noble, Lord of the great throne, by His beautiful names and lofty attributes to write for all of us firmness and guidance to His straight path; and to save us from the path of those that earned His anger and the path of the misguided and to rectify our situation and to rectify our religion, which is the preservation of our affairs, and to rectify our Dunya that we live in and to rectify our hereafter which is our return and make our lives an increase in every kind of good and our deaths a final respite from every kind of evil.

Our final call is to the praise of Allāh Lord of all creation.

And may the prayers, peace and blessings be upon the

---

[68] Al-Ahqaaf [46:13-14]

servant of Allāh, His messenger and prophet, Muhammad,
and upon his family and companions

Printed in Great Britain
by Amazon

42231157R00031